ARCHITECTURE OF THE ANCIENT ONES

Architecture of the Ancient Ones

PHOTOGRAPHY BY VAL BRINKERHOFF
TEXT BY A. DUDLEY GARDNER

GIBBS·SMITH
P
PUBLISHER

SALT LAKE CITY

Circular Ruin with Varnish and Handprints,
Colorado Plateau, A.D. 1300.
This small round structure with painted figures
and nearby handprints is juxtaposed against
the natural design of desert varnish on a tall
cliff side, adjoining a large natural-stone
bridge. The deep canyon setting is magical.
The purpose of the small ruin is unknown.

First Edition
05 04 03 02 01 00   5 4 3 2 1

Photographs © 2000 by Val Brinkerhoff
Text © 2000 by Gibbs Smith, Publisher

Published by
Gibbs Smith, Publisher
P.O. Box 667
Layton, Utah 84041

To order: (1-800) 748-5439
E-mail: info@gibbs-smith.com
Web site: www.gibbs-smith.com

Edited by Suzanne Taylor
Designed by J. Scott Knudsen, Park City, Utah
Printed and bound in Korea

Library of Congress Cataloging-in-Publication Data

Brinkerhoff, Val, 1956–
    Architecture of the Ancient Ones / photographs by Val
Brinkerhoff; text by A. Dudley Gardner.—1st ed.
    p. cm.
ISBN 0-87905-955-9
    1. Pueblo architecture. 2. Pueblo Indians—Social life
    and customs. I. Gardner, A. Dudley. II. Title.
E99.P9 B725 2000
720′.979—dc21
                    99-057372

Infectious Beauty

Whether it is the red sunrises, the fire in the sky at dusk, or the shimmering mirages in the heat of the day, there is a beauty in the Southwest that ties the imagination to the land. It is an ancient land where the discovery of stone tools proves that people have lived in the region for thousands of years. The items left behind and the sandstone cliffs cutting across the sky convey a sense of endless expanses, but the cliff dwellings and empty kivas show that in a land of apparently limitless vistas, there are endings. The contradiction is haunting, and the empty kivas, open spaces, and the sunset capture hearts and souls, drawing visitors back to the Southwest, seeking new places and old remains of stone villages and homes.

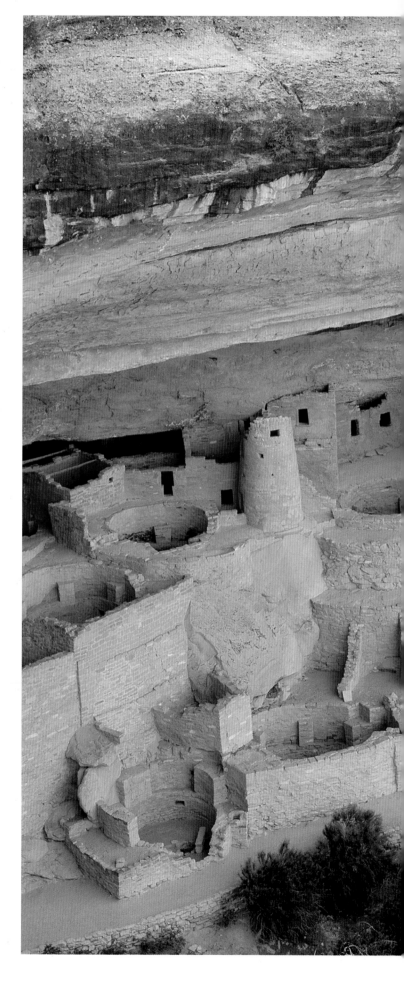

Cliff Palace, Mesa Verde National Park, Colorado, A.D. 1200. Protected by dry climate and its high, remote canyon location, these 800-year-old ruins represent some of the most magical architectural treasures in North America. Here Cliff Palace presents stunning buildings, once housing as many as 250 people.

*M*arie Wormington, one of the Southwest's first women archaeologists, understood the attraction of the region's land and heritage. She wrote a history describing the lives of the Indians in the Southwest based on archaeological facts. Of the land, she said she awoke one morning and the place owned her, owned her in the sense that she needed to return there to work and feel at home. Marie wrote: "There is something infectious about the Southwest. Some are immune to it, but there are others who have no resistance to the subtle vistas and who must spend the rest of their lives dreaming of the incredible sweep of the desert, of great golden mesas with purple shadows, and tremendous stars appearing at dusk from a turquoise sky." She added that once infected by the Southwest, "there is nothing one can do but strive to return again and again."

[1] H. M. Wormington, *Prehistoric Indians of the Southwest* (Denver: The Denver Museum of Natural History, 1970), 3. Reprinted by permission of the Denver Museum of Natural History.

Kiva and Two-Story Ruin, Ute Mountain Tribal Park, Colorado, A.D. 1140. Nestled beneath a massive yellow sandstone alcove in the high canyons of southwestern Colorado, this tall structure features a round once-covered kiva, a center for social and religious activity.

ray Marcos, one of the first
Europeans to see the Zuni
pueblos, was so struck by the
golden canyons and Zuni
homes that he thought he had
seen the Seven Golden Cities of Cibola, a land
of Spanish myth, where the streets were paved
with gold and the houses made from precious
metals. Fray Marcos never did see the fabled
cities; he made up a story to impress the king.
So believable was Marcos's tale that Coronado
came north in 1540 seeking the cities. He
found, instead, the beauty of the pueblos and
mesas, a land of rich cultural heritage.

**Fallen Roof Ruin, Horizontal, Colorado
Plateau, A.D. 1200.**
This striking three-room ruin sits beneath an
unusual roof structure composed of sandstone
and whitish alkaline deposits. The setting of
the ruin in a small alcove high atop a remote
canyon cliff face, along with its construction
beneath the abstract ceiling, creates a dramatic
juxtaposition of form, color, and texture.

Wukoki Ruin, Wupatki National Monument, Arizona, A.D. 1100.
Surrounded by the harsh desert landscape of the Wupatki Basin near Sunset Crater, the Ancient Ones of this area utilized a fine blanket of cinder and ash for farming. Spewn from a nearby volcano in 1605, this covering helped desert soils retain moisture.

THE ANCIENT ONES

The Anasazi, as the cliff dwellers were once called, were excellent farmers. They cultivated corn, beans, and squash. In some places they irrigated their lands, and in others they took advantage of the summer monsoons that carried rains and life into the desert. To successfully raise food, the rains needed to fall at the right time of year. To ensure this, the "Ancient Ones," as the Anasazi are now known, called on their ancestors from the underworld to bring the waters from heaven to their fields.

One myth held by the Ancient Ones was that all the people once lived in the underworld, a world below the earth's surface that was much like ours but free from problems and diseases. These inhabitants found a way out onto the surface through an opening called a *sipapu*. Through this climbed the Ancient Ones, the founders of the human race. But one day a coyote, a trickster, found the sipapu and covered it with stone. Since millions of stones cover the Southwest,

finding the specific stone that covered the sipapu proved impossible, and the path to the underworld was closed forever. Now a barrier existed between the ancestors and those on the surface.

After that, the people in the above world had to communicate with those in the underworld to ensure the rains fell and harmony continued. This need had a profound effect on the Ancient Ones, as well as the Hopi and Zuni, who lived much like the cliff dwellers. To them their land was the center of the universe.

To talk to the ancestors, the Ancient Ones built kivas with sipapus. For some cultures the sipapu symbolized the connection to the underworld, while the circular kiva symbolized the universe. Kivas built below ground were not abandoned by the Ancient Ones when they moved out of Mesa Verde or Chaco. According to legend, the spirits of the ancestors continue to live in the cliff dwellings. In the minds of the Pueblo Indians in the Southwest, the Ancient Ones' souls inhabit the remains of the kivas.

Balcony House, Mesa Verde National Park, Colorado, A.D. 1200.
Located six hundred feet above the canyon floor, Balcony House sits dramatically at the edge of a deep mesa canyon facing east. Most cliff dwellings face south, providing needed warmth from the winter sun. At the back of the ruin, a sacred spring provides water. Tree-ring dating indicates that the last timbers for Balcony house were cut in A.D. 1282, making it one of the last ruins abandoned at Mesa Verde. Climatic changes, deforestation, and a prolonged drought are thought to have combined to force the abandonment of such archaeological treasures.

While the economy of the Ancient Ones centered around raising corn, squash, and beans, planting corn also reflected a dependence on the ancestors. Seeds were placed in the ground, from where the ancestors appeared. Seeds were dropped into the soil when the sun's yearly cycle marked that spring had arrived on the mesas. At that time, villagers gathered in the fields and, before they planted, smoked their pipes and prayed to the gods and ancestors for help. After placing prayer sticks (a sacred bundle of string and feathers) on the ground in front of a shrine located along the edges of each field, a holy man sprinkled a handful of ground corn on the shrine and prayed for rain. The prayer also included a plea for good crops, the basis of survival for Pueblo societies.

Sunset, Prayer Circle #2,
Colorado Plateau, A.D. 1300.
This round, kiva-like structure, with
south-facing entrance, sits upon a
fifteen-hundred-foot-tall, twenty-foot
wide sandstone butte. The view of the
canyon lands in the distance is peaceful
and majestic yet haunting.

Sunrise, Prayer Circle #3,
Colorado Plateau, A.D. 1300.
Circular in shape, like the ceremonial kivas
found throughout the ruins of the Southwest,
this structure sits high atop a very tall thin
butte overlooking the rugged canyon lands
of the Colorado Plateau. The purpose of such
structures is unknown, but their beautiful
and precarious settings can produce feelings
of awe and reverence.

STRUCTURES

The majority of the cliff dwellings, pueblos, granaries, and other structures were constructed to blend into the surrounding land. Houses, kivas, and granaries were primarily made from local material: stones from nearby sandstone and mud from the valley floors.

Sandstone and mud found nearby was used to form the walls. Mud served as plaster for both the interior and exterior walls. The roofs were made with wood from juniper, piñon, cottonwood, or pine trees. Some trees were nearby while others had to be hauled long distances. The timber was used to form the ceilings of houses, and if a room was built above the structure, the wood ceiling doubled as a floor. The timbers were supported by the walls, and the logs held the structure together. The construction was masterful in its simplicity. The combination of stones, mud, and wood created buildings that have endured centuries and blend beautifully into the land.

Fire Roof Ruin, Colorado Plateau, A.D. 1200.
Carefully constructed below this fire-like canyon overhang, this small but dramatic ruin showcases the expert ability of the Ancient Ones in blending their architecture into the surrounding stone with great aesthetic awareness.

Fallen Roof Ruin, Vertical, Colorado Plateau, A.D. 1200.
Nestled under a magical roof of orange sandstone in a small cliff alcove deep in canyon country, this three-room ruin demonstrates the desire of the Ancient Ones to build in places of great visual power and presence. Most cliff dwellings also feature beautiful views and grand vistas of the surrounding desert or canyon landscape, making the pilgrimage to such sites even more enchanting.

Granary or Small Ruin, Cedar Mesa, Utah, A.D. 1200.
Small flat sandstone doors measuring approximately twelve by eighteen inches are often found near more-remote ruin and granary sites and were used to keep out the weather and hungry animals. Typical of most structures of the Ancient Ones is the aesthetic integration of the structure within the natural landscape.

Storing corn for future use required the construction of granaries. Some of these were large structures built within the pueblos. Others were tucked into rock outcroppings, or canyon walls or under stone overhangs. The architecture was integrated into the surrounding stone, creating an aesthetically pleasing construction. The hive-shaped structures were large enough to hold several hundred bushels of corn but small enough to remain hidden. They were sealed shut, and mud covered the exterior. Today the smooth mud exteriors contain handprints, while the interiors have the imprints of corncobs. Form followed a function, and some artists have described the simple beauty of a stone granary as magical in its ability to convey art through a functional structure nestled silently in a cliff face or under a rock outcrop.

Although the Ancient Ones' economy centered around raising corn, squash, and beans, they developed a sophisticated culture capable of building dwelling houses so large that equivalents were not seen until the twentieth century. Chaco's walls in northwestern New Mexico still tower above the desert floor. In southwestern Colorado, people built houses on the green tables that rise above the valley floor, but some moved down off the high mesas into the rock shelters in the cliffs. Some archaeologists contend they moved off the mesas to acquire more area to farm; others say it was to be closer to the water flowing from springs. But most feel that in setting their home in rock shelters, the Ancient Ones could better defend their homes.

Dwelling, Comb Ridge, Utah, A.D. 1200. Many small granaries and habitations are found throughout the Four Corners area beneath small canyon overhangs, where interesting natural-rock features make for an appropriate construction setting in terms of both aesthetics and physical comfort. Here a lantern was used to simulate the look of fire used by the Ancient Ones.

The rock shelters also protected them from the elements. The cliff dwellings were ideally situated to take advantage of the sun and shade. In the winter, the cliffs served as solar reservoirs: the rocks absorbed the sun's heat and radiated it back into the shelter through the night. In the summer, the shaded areas deep in the cliffs kept the air cool. As a result, elaborate structures emerged there. Places like Cliff Palace in Mesa Verde National Park contained rooms, kivas, and plazas, all tucked into beautiful red sandstone. And at Crow Canyon, west of Mesa Verde, elaborate villages appeared along mesa sides, all built by people whose economy depended on the spirits sending summer rains.

**Moonhouse Ruin Complex,
Colorado Plateau, A.D. 1300.**
This remote, well-preserved, apartment-like ruin site features a variety of room blocks, each with distinctive doorways or windows. At left an unusual windowsill once allowed inhabitants to view out over the impressive canyon below, where deer and other animals, as well as hostile enemies, may have resided. Vandalism has recently marred precious artifacts, such as the metate in the foreground, which was used to grind corn. Care must be taken when visiting such sites to preserve their beauty and history for future generations.

Ruins, Keet Seel, Navajo National Monument,
Arizona, A.D. 1200.
Keet Seel features some of the best-preserved
ancient architecture in the Southwest. Majestically
nestled beneath an impressive sandstone cliff with
desert varnish lines of great beauty, this ruin
contains over 150 rooms, most of which have
original roof structures intact. Here the building
materials of the Ancient Ones are exposed for
investigation.

Throughout the Southwest thousands of structures exist that were built by the Ancient Ones. A variety of stone structures are spread across the remote reaches of the region. Some are intimate and inviting, others are monumental and awe inspiring. The stone buildings are artistic monuments to the efforts of people building with the materials at hand. Many of the structures survived because they were built under rock overhangs away from the elements. Detailed stonework and deft rock carving created walls that stood over time. As the stones weathered and the lichens grew on the buildings, the dwellings and the land began to appear as one. The small pueblos became like an inlay, gracefully fastened to the rock floors under the sandstone roofs. The rock shelters and smaller cliff dwellings became aesthetic blends of nature and human design. Most of the stone homes have only been seen by a few people because they lie in remote silent canyons.

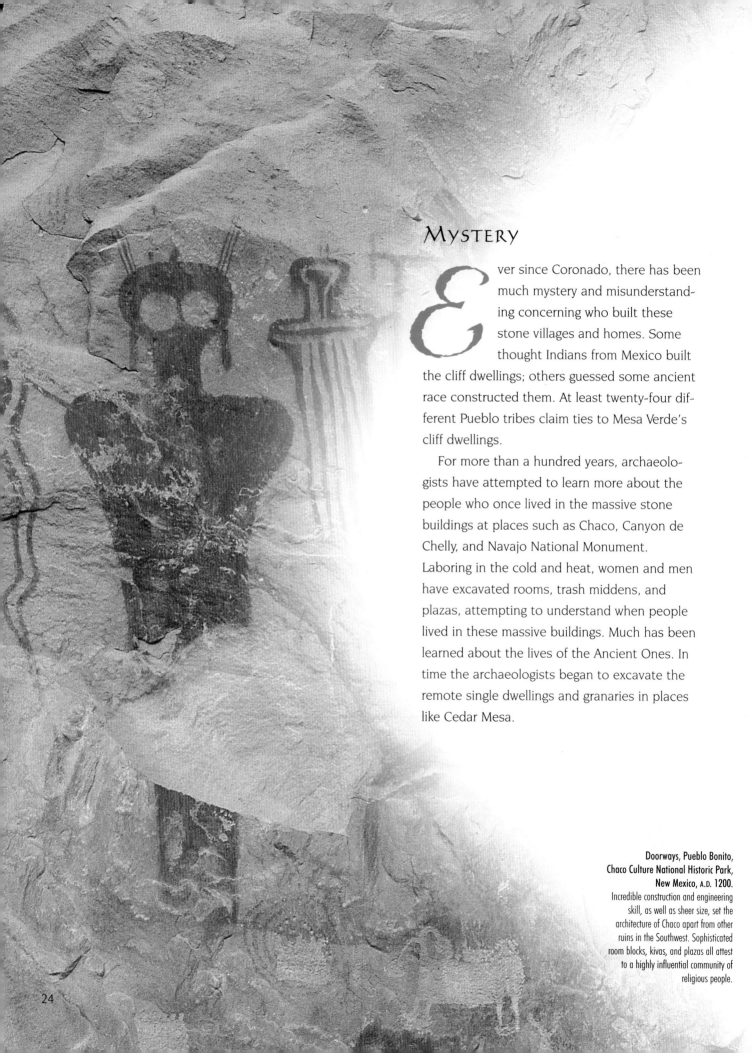

MYSTERY

Ever since Coronado, there has been much mystery and misunderstanding concerning who built these stone villages and homes. Some thought Indians from Mexico built the cliff dwellings; others guessed some ancient race constructed them. At least twenty-four different Pueblo tribes claim ties to Mesa Verde's cliff dwellings.

For more than a hundred years, archaeologists have attempted to learn more about the people who once lived in the massive stone buildings at places such as Chaco, Canyon de Chelly, and Navajo National Monument. Laboring in the cold and heat, women and men have excavated rooms, trash middens, and plazas, attempting to understand when people lived in these massive buildings. Much has been learned about the lives of the Ancient Ones. In time the archaeologists began to excavate the remote single dwellings and granaries in places like Cedar Mesa.

Doorways, Pueblo Bonito, Chaco Culture National Historic Park, New Mexico, A.D. 1200.
Incredible construction and engineering skill, as well as sheer size, set the architecture of Chaco apart from other ruins in the Southwest. Sophisticated room blocks, kivas, and plazas all attest to a highly influential community of religious people.

Twin Towers, Ute Mountain Ute Tribal Park, Colorado, A.D. **1200.**
These two small structures may have been used as granaries or for habitation. Located just south of Mesa Verde National Park in Lion Canyon, the Ute Tribal Park Ruins remain in a more rustic natural condition without the rebuilding and beautification seen in national parks such as Chaco Canyon or Mesa Verde.

Above right: **Window, Sill, and Metates, Moonhouse Ruin Complex, Colorado Plateau**, A.D. **1200.**
The remnants of two large corn-grinding stones, or metates, are seen here beneath an unusual window with braced windowsill. The exterior wall of this structure is made from six-foot poles covered with mud, sticks, and paint stripes. The deep dry alcove setting has preserved the site for eight hundred years of harsh desert weather.

Preceding page: **Keet Seel Ruin, Navajo National Monument, Arizona**, A.D. **1200.**
Containing one hundred and fifty rooms and six kivas, Keet Seel (a Navajo word for "broken pottery") is one of the best-preserved and most-impressive ruin sites in North America. Discovered by Richard Wetherill with the aid of a Navajo guide in 1895, it was established as a national monument in 1909 by President William H. Taft. The massive alcove ruin site was deserted in A.D. 1300.

There is much debate about when the Ancient Ones began to farm in the Four Corners area, a modern term for the section where Arizona, Colorado, New Mexico, and Utah meet. (For the Ancient Ones it was often where Ship Rock to the south, Monument Valley to the west, Ute Mountain to the east, and Blue Mountain to the north could be seen.) Into this region came farmers and builders. There is a generalized sequence of events that define how the Ancient Ones' culture evolved. At Bat Cave, in south-western New Mexico, corn dating to 1000 B.C. has been found. As a result of recent work in New Mexico and Arizona, archaeologists contend that corn appeared in the Southwest between 2000 B.C. and 1800 B.C. Some scientists feel the latter date reflects the first cultivation of corn in the United States. The former date still reflects that corn was grown in the Southwest at an earlier date than first believed. Archaeologists believe that the rise of Pueblo societies began with the more intensive reliance on corn for food. What is important is the rise in the dependence on agriculture as a primary source of food.

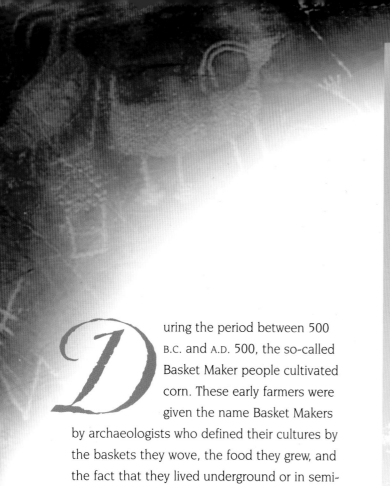

During the period between 500 B.C. and A.D. 500, the so-called Basket Maker people cultivated corn. These early farmers were given the name Basket Makers by archaeologists who defined their cultures by the baskets they wove, the food they grew, and the fact that they lived underground or in semi-subterranean pit houses. There is a debate among archaeologists about when the dependence on corn increased. Some hold that agriculture was adopted by indigenous hunters and gatherers. Others put forth the idea that emigrants from southern Arizona and New Mexico brought corn north to the Ancient Ones' homeland. Most archaeologists, however, believe that hunters and gatherers in the Four Corners area adopted the farming methods needed to raise maize. By Basket Maker times, farming had become part of the southwestern landscape.

Small Ruin, Poncho House Ruin Complex, Navajo Reservation, Colorado Plateau, A.D. 1200.
The ruins at Poncho House are both magical and practical, showcasing the desire of the Ancient Ones to integrate their architecture into the natural surroundings in an aesthetic fashion. The south-facing exposure provides both warmth from winter sun and an impressive view of the Monument Valley area to the southwest. Standing eerily quiet today, this large ruin complex was once full of bustling activity, as evidenced by the thousands of pot shards spread below at the cliff base.

The increasing dependence on the cultivation of beans, squash, and corn led to the rise of the Pueblo cultures in the Southwest. One theory states that, beginning about the time of Christ, farmers began to cultivate more intensively in some areas within the Southwest. While the date when farming began varied from place to place, there are some generalized dates that mark the rise of agriculture in the Southwest. As early as A.D. 500, a transition in the nature of the Basket Maker society was under way. It is possible that the use of new strains of corn seed and improved farming methods helped increase crop yields. Corn and squash still sustained the society, but the increased crop yields permitted a population growth that led to further modification in the Basket Maker culture. Around A.D. 700, that transition was nearly complete.

Horsecollar Ruin, Colorado Plateau, A.D. 1300.
Lit by lantern and warm sunlight, this distinctive mud-and-sandstone structure features two small adjoining rooms with horse-collar-shaped doorways. The Ancient Ones utilized fire for light, warmth, cooking, and the making of pottery.

DEVELOPMENT

The early pueblo phase that began in A.D. 700 was marked by the abandonment of underground homes or pit houses in favor of houses on the surface. In some areas this transition may have begun at an earlier date. By the mid-800s, stone structures were built with rooms situated side by side to form larger dwellings. In time some dwellings featured multiple levels. The farmers still retained their subterranean structures, which served as kivas for ceremonial rites. In fact, at Chaco around A.D. 900, Pueblo Bonito appeared in its infant form. By around A.D. 1000 in some locations, these dwellings and ceremonial structures had become elaborate complexes. While the mesas were densely populated in some places, some of the Ancient Ones began to move off the mesas into cliff shelters. By A.D. 1100 cliff dwellings began to appear. Between A.D. 900 and 1200, the larger structures at Chaco, Mesa Verde, and Canyon de Chelly had been completed.

Doorways, West Wing, Aztec Ruins National Monument, New Mexico, A.D. 1200.
The construction style at Aztec shows influence from the peoples at Mesa Verde, forty miles to the northwest, and at Chaco Canyon, fifty miles to the south. Early pioneers misnamed Aztec, thinking that the sophisticated construction was the work of their ancient Mexican neighbors to the south.

Square Tower House, Mesa Verde National Park, Colorado, A.D. 1200.
Over four thousand prehistoric sites are found at the Mesa Verde site. Constructed as early as A.D. 800, most of the six hundred cliff dwellings were built in the thirteenth century. This four-story tower may have been used for defensive purposes after the Ancient Ones moved down into the canyons from the mesa tops.

**Doorway, Pueblo Bonito,
Chaco Culture National Historic Park,
New Mexico, A.D. 1100.**
With over eight hundred rooms and rising as
high as five stories, the D-shaped Pueblo
Bonito features architecture of great skill and
curiosity. Large plazas, great kivas, huge
room blocks, and striking passages all attest
to the development of Anasazi culture. Here,
cool blue skylight in the foreground contrasts
with warm reflected sunlight in the distance.
T-shaped doorways may have been useful for
carrying large shoulder-supported loads in
and out of the structures.

Montezuma's Castle, Montezuma Castle National Monument, Arizona, A.D. 1200. Curved to conform to the arc of the surrounding cliff alcove, this five-story fortress was built by the Sinagua in the 1100s and contains seventeen rooms. Unlike most Anasazi sandstone ruins, the Castle is made of small limestone blocks laid in mud mortar. The roof was constructed using large sycamore timbers covered by poles, grass, small sticks, and then more mud. As with most ruin sites, a nearby water source (Beaver Creek) was a must.

While the Ancient Ones built their pueblos and kivas, the Hohokam of southern Arizona and Mogollon in south and central New Mexico developed their own sophisticated cultures. Hohokam canals can still be seen in southern Arizona. These water-filled arteries proved to be the lifeblood of the culture. Using irrigation, the desert bloomed and large towns appeared. Meanwhile, the Mogollon people to the east built pueblos and kivas and agricultural systems that relied on summer rains to irrigate their fields. The Mogollon and Hohokam, while similar to their neighbors in the Four Corners area, had distinctive cultures. Examples of these differences are illustrated in their pottery and kivas.

Both the Ancient Ones and the Mogollon people built their kivas underground, complete

Wupatki Pueblo, Wupatki National Monument, Arizona, A.D. 1100.
This dwelling site features a rare masonry ball court nestled between two ruin sites, not far from Sunset Crater, a volcano that erupted in 1065. The resulting fine blanket of cinders and ash upon the surrounding inhospitable landscape made farming possible since the volcanic covering insulated moisture. This Sinagua site showcases influences from both the Anasazi and the Hohokam.

with deflectors and sipapus. The deflectors helped spread the fire's heat evenly throughout the structure. The sipapu connected the ancestors to the world above. Unlike their neighbors farther north at Mesa Verde and Cedar Mesa who built circular places of worship, most Mogollon built rectangular kivas.

At Astinna, south of the Zuni Mountains in northern New Mexico, the inhabitants of the pueblo constructed both a rectangular and circular kiva. The circular kiva lies to the south, facing the Mogollon. The rectangular one sits to the north, facing the homes of the Ancient Ones. A path runs between the two kivas, symbolizing that the worlds of the Mogollon and Ancient Ones were not that far apart. It's also possible that the two kivas connect the older circular Mogollon pit houses with their new rectangular kivas.

There is little doubt that the Ancient Ones, the Hohokam, and the Mogollon were influenced by the advanced cultures in Mexico. Macaw feathers from parrots in Mexico have been found in ruins from southern New Mexico to Colorado. In Mexico, turquoise from outcrops in New Mexico and Arizona have been found in graves.

Turquoise beads and small squares used as decoration traveled south, and pottery and feathers traveled north from places like Casa Grande in northern Mexico. The builders of the great kivas at Chaco apparently had direct trade links to the city builders in Mexico. These trade connections would have given the pueblo dwellers an awareness of some of the world's

greatest civilizations. North Americans, long before Europeans arrived, possessed knowledge of the region's resources.

From about A.D. 900 to 1300, pueblos and granaries were constructed throughout the Southwest. Some of the structures, such as those at Mesa Verde, Aztec National Monument, and Chaco Canyon, were massive. From about 900 to 1125, Chaco dominated the region. About 1110 the power was transferred north near the San Juan River where Aztec was constructed. The people of Aztec dominated the area from 1110 to 1275. Meanwhile, farther north, in the canyon walls of Mesa Verde, the cliff dwellers reached their zenith as builders. But these were not the only buildings being built.

Ruins, Aztec Ruins National Monument, New Mexico, A.D. 1200.
These misnamed ruins were occupied by two separate Anasazi groups: the first closely allied to the people of Chaco Canyon in the early 1100s, and the second to Mesa Verde occupants in the early 1200s. Aztec features the remnants of highly religious people expressed via thirty kivas, one of which is massive and unique among all Anasazi culture.

Above left: **Massive Kiva, Chetro Ketl, Chaco Culture National Historic Park, New Mexico, A.D. 1200.**
Once covered by a large roof supported by huge timbers anchored in the four visible round slots, this impressive kiva was one of many used primarily by men as centers for religious and social gatherings.

Stronghold House, Hovenweep National Monument, Utah, A.D. 1200.
Built atop a sandstone outcropping in a shallow canyon on the Cajon Mesa, this ruin may have been used as a defensive lookout or for studying the heavens. By A.D. 1300 this and other Hovenweep structures were deserted.

hroughout the Four Corners
area, small stone-built farmsteads and smaller pueblos
began to appear. The towers at
Hovenweep and smaller pueb-
los in the cliff shelters along Cedar Mesa in
present-day Utah were built at the same time.
Removed from the larger pueblos, the farmsteads
housed cultivators in the summer. The remains of
these smaller dwellings are as impressive in their
construction as the larger structures, often blending into the natural landscape.

Both small and large structures were built
into the cliff sides, where generations of children played and grew to adulthood.

From cliff perches above the valley floors, the
builders of the cliff dwellings and their children
could see into the vast reaches of the valleys.
Cliff dwellers could climb down to canyon
streams or up to the mesa tops where corn and
beans grew. Cornfields were scattered over the
mesas and on the valley floors to take advantage of available moisture. While little is known
about the day-to-day lives of children in the
pueblos, toys have been uncovered by archaeologists, showing that children played in the
plazas and near their homes.

Holly Group, Hovenweep National Monument, Colorado, A.D. 1200.
Hovenweep is a Ute Indian word for "deserted valley," and features six clusters of very unusual, castle-like structures on the Utah-Colorado border. Each sits at the head of a box canyon, reminding modern-day visitors that these curious constructions may have been used for habitation, ceremonial purposes, observing the enemy, or studying the heavens.

PLACES OF PEACE

There is a charm in going to the abandoned pueblos and walking quietly where others lived. It is easy to believe that children once played there. It is harder to know why the builders constructed their homes in cliffs and built towers above the mesas. Looking at how historians and archaeologists viewed these builders is informative.

Historical views as to why the Ancient Ones built homes at Hovenweep, Mesa Verde, or on the Cedar Mesa have varied. Traditionally, historians and archaeologists have viewed the builders of the pueblos favorably. Some saw the pueblo inhabitants as yeomen farmers producing something akin to democratic societies. Other historians have seen them as peaceful cultures. But modern archaeologists have begun to view the pueblo period between A.D. 1100 and 1500 as a time fraught with warfare and strife. Citing the construction of defensive towers and protective cliff dwellings, modern revisionist historians presented a view of the region that is not at all peaceful. There are examples of rock art and pottery that depict warriors and battles, and there are graves in the Four Corners area that contain burned and battered bodies, evidence that some of the pueblos may have been built for protection.

Nonetheless, no matter how the views of the past change, the magnificent structures left behind by the architects of Hovenweep and Chaco Canyon indicate that an advanced culture once lived in the Southwest, one that provides modern visitors with places of peace to seek solitude—quite the opposite of what may have happened historically.

Betatakin Ruins, Navajo National Monument, Arizona, A.D. 1260.
Constructed along a long ledge beneath a massive five-hundred-foot-high cliff overhang, this impressive ruin site was inhabited by the Kayenta Anasazi for only thirty years. Strong summer thunderstorms may have caused damaging arroyo cutting, which, when combined with later drought, may have forced the Ancient Ones farther south. Betatakin, Navajo for "ledge house," was discovered by John Wetherill in 1907.

Mummy Cave Ruin Complex, Canyon de Chelly National Monument, Arizona, A.D. 1200.
Inhabited for some two thousand years, Canyon de Chelly features colorful one-thousand-foot-high sandstone cliff faces that provide a dramatic backdrop for numerous fascinating dwelling and rock-art sites. Here the hauntingly beautiful Mummy Cave is situated between two cliff alcoves.

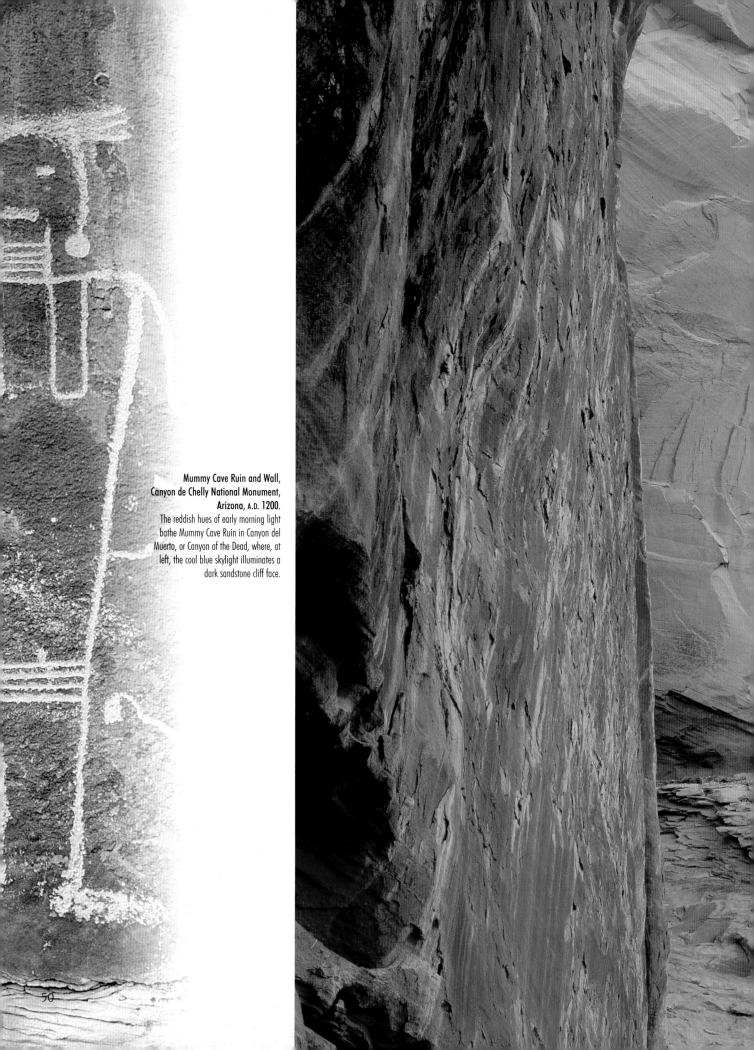

**Mummy Cave Ruin and Wall,
Canyon de Chelly National Monument,
Arizona, A.D. 1200.**
The reddish hues of early morning light
bathe Mummy Cave Ruin in Canyon del
Muerto, or Canyon of the Dead, where, at
left, the cool blue skylight illuminates a
dark sandstone cliff face.

TRACES

While few written records of the Ancient Ones remain, the art of the region survives. There is little known about the people's hopes and dreams, but the fingerprints in mud and paint tie us to their humanity and labors in remote canyons and mesas.

The stone walls of the buildings were often covered inside and out with mud plaster. In kivas and elsewhere, the walls might have been painted with designs or figures of animals and humans. The painters used the mud plaster as their canvas. Today few examples of these designs remain, as the mud has dissolved with centuries of rain and wind. Where they survive, the effect is striking.

At a place called El Morro, the ancient pueblos and prehistoric stones are covered with images made by the Ancient Ones and the Spanish. El Morro rises as a white sandstone mark on the historic trail between Zuni and Acoma Pueblos. The presence of a permanent water source at El Morro made the area a magnet for travelers passing along the natural transportation corridor between the Rio Grande and the Flagstaff Mountains in northern Arizona. Prehistoric transportation and trade networks were extensive, and the trail that passed by El Morro was tied into a network that reached Mexico. The natural corridor north of El Morro was used by the first occupants in the area.

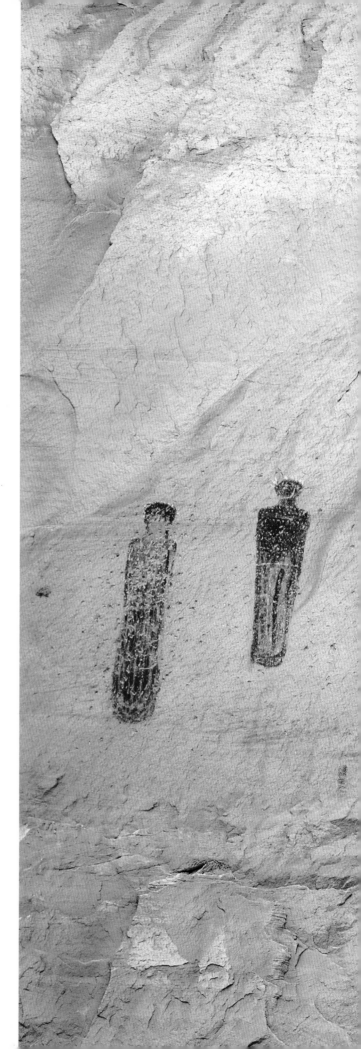

Pictographs, Horseshoe Canyon Annex, Canyonlands National Park, Utah, A.D. 400. Entitled "The Holy Ghost Group," these nine-feet-tall, Barrier Canyon—style pictographs (paint on rock image) are both impressive and haunting. Stylized and possibly representing a shaman-like leader, spirit, or god surrounded by individuals of lesser standing, these pictographs are most likely archaic or pre-Anasazi, dating to approximately A.D. 400. Although their true meaning is unknown, their purpose may have been ceremonial, decorative, religious, artistic, or as a warning for those entering sacred ground.

ℰl Morro became significant because it possessed water adjacent to a major transportation corridor. As the water attracted the Native American inhabitants, the stone walls became a canvas on which human and animal figures were carved.

In some of the ruins, walls are decorated with handprints, made by tracing the hands, or in some cases by dipping the hands in paint and applying it to the wall. In other instances the hands were set on the stone while paint or powder was blown around them.

The pottery and rock art of the Ancient Ones conveys a small sense of what the builders of the pueblos thought and felt. The handprints painted or pecked into rock walls or drawn on pots help us touch the past. The visible tie between the past and the present is carried through the recognizable animals depicted by the builders of the pueblos. Human hands seem to transcend time and culture, linking us to the land, knowing that in the distant past another person stood here and looked at this place and touched this stone.

Handprints and Ruin, Colorado Plateau, A.D. 1200.
Handprints and other forms of rock art are often found near many ruin sites throughout the Four Corners region. Here the Ancient Ones used natural strawlike plant stalks to blow white pigment around their hands from atop the roof of the ruin.

Hand Pictograph, Colorado Plateau,
A.D. **1100.**
The Ancient Ones dipped their hands in mud or pigments and "marked" areas surrounding their dwellings. In order to preserve these, travelers to such sites should be careful not to touch them.

The prehistoric inscriptions at El Morro and the pueblo atop the white stone-faced mesa were significant cultural features that led to the creation of El Morro National Park. But for the visitor it is often the combination of the historical remnants and the land itself that makes El Morro unique. Visitors to the park gain a sense of timelessness as they look across the endless view between Atsinna atop El Morro and the Zuni Mountains to the north—a world little changed since the 1500s. But this sense of time and place have begun to erode as development on the fringes of the monument comes within view of El Morro.

Warrior Petroglyph, Dinosaur National Park, Utah, A.D. **1000.** Located far north of the Ancient Ones, this Fremont Indian warrior petroglyph (image carved into rock), contrasts dramatically with those of the more peaceful Anasazi to the south, who relied primarily on farming for their sustenance. This fierce figure may be holding the head of his victim at right. Petroglyphs such as this one may have been used to ward off enemies or uninvited travelers.

**Remote Cliff Ruin,
Colorado Plateau, A.D. 1200.**
Deep into the high canyons of the Four
Corners area lie many undisturbed ruin sites
in pristine condition. Here many original
artifacts are intact, including the flat stone
used to cover the window or doorway,
keeping out wind, sun, water, and invaders.
The ruin is in remarkable condition due to
its remoteness and its physical location
beneath a high, dry desert cliff overhang.

At El Morro the lichen on the stones and the massive cliffs rising high above the valley floor bear the slowly worn scars of nature and the marks of a people who spent a few minutes or hours carving their names. Names and dates fix people and time at this point beneath the massive cliffs. Against the backdrop of the Zuni Mountains and ever-changing sky, the cliffs are tied to the slow processes of geological forces. They carry dates spanning four centuries, but they also reflect the slow motion of geological time. Though the rock cliffs were there before humans arrived, the names embedded on their walls connect modern visitors with the Indians, Spaniards, Mexicans, military detachments, and westward-bound emigrants.

Caveate, Puyé Cliff Dwellings, New Mexico, A.D. 1300.
Once fronted by masonry rooms, this small cave dwelling was dug from a two-story cliff face of tuff, a lightweight porous volcanic rock that is easily shaped with simple stone tools. Green lichens and blue skylight provide brilliant color to the grayish-white cliffs, which are dotted with similar ruins and plant life.

61

ABANDONMENT

For generations the travelers to Chaco Canyon, Mesa Verde, and Cedar Mesa have wondered what happened to the people who built such massive monuments and carved detailed pictures into the stone faces of cliffs. Where did they go? This is one of the least-agreed-upon topics in southwestern archaeology.

Between A.D. 1400 and 1500, the great pueblos were abandoned. Their inhabitants scattered throughout the region, some moving to the Rio Grande to build elaborate pueblos along the river valley, others, such as the ancestors of the Hopi and Zuni, moving to northeastern Arizona or northwestern New Mexico. But there are no clear indications as to why they left the cliff dwellings.

Whitehouse Ruin, Canyon de Chelly National Monument, Arizona, A.D. 1200. Housing approximately one hundred inhabitants from A.D. 1060 to 1275, Whitehouse Ruin sits at the base of colorful sheer sandstone cliffs in beautiful Canyon de Chelly, Arizona. The canyon has been the home of Anasazi, Hopi, and Navajo for over two thousand years and contains seven hundred prehistoric sites, including striking rock art, all among great natural beauty and working Navajo farms along the canyon bottoms.

One of the most widely accepted views is that there was a major change in the environment that made farming the region no longer viable. The rings of trees found in roof beams of the abandoned pueblos indicate that at the end of the classical pueblo period less rain fell, though some scientists point out that not all tree rings denote a region-wide drought. In response to this, other archaeologists have contended that indeed there was adequate moisture in some places but that the water at the terminal period of the pueblos came in the form of winter snow. In this latter case, growing seasons may have shortened and crops would not have matured properly. Without large dams the spring runoff from snowmelt could not have been stored for summer use. There are numerous explanations, but some questions remain unanswered.

Poncho House and Cliff Face, Navajo Reservation, Colorado Plateau, A.D. 1200. Majestically constructed into the alcove base of an impressive cliff face, this large and unusual ruin site is bathed in the warm light of a summer sunset. Like most Anasazi cliff dwellings, the juxtaposition of the architecture within the surrounding rock reveals a concern for both aesthetics and practicality.

Past researchers theorized that invading peoples pushed the Ancient Ones from their homelands. But this explanation often puts forth the idea that the ancestors of the modern Apache and Navajo drove the Pueblo people from their homes. Archaeological evidence indicates the Apache and Navajo arrived after the pueblos were abandoned. Others doubt this because the Pueblo population outnumbered their successors. Others hold that raiders from the south instead of from the north drove the people from their homes.

The more one looks, the more explanations one finds as to why the great societies of the Ancient Ones vanished. Some contend that environmental degradation led to the people leaving their mesas and traveling to the Rio Grande. It's possible that the soils were over-tilled and the nutrients depleted. One theory has it that the forests at Mesa Verde were completely cut down and there was no longer a source of wood for fuel and construction. Another idea asks: Did the end of the great societies come about due to European diseases preceding the arrival of the Spaniards, or due to some other type of biological malady? All of these theories have their supporters and detractors. What we do know is the buildings were abandoned and the fields left uncultivated. The people did not vanish, however, because they are the ancestors of the modern Pueblo cultures in New Mexico and Arizona. What remain are the hauntingly beautiful shells of empty stone homes built by ancient people on an ancient land.

Alcove Ruin, Butler Wash, Utah, A.D. 1200.
Nestled in a small cliff-face cave, this small ruin sits beneath a fire-blackened roof and features a fencelike masonry wall preceding the slope of the cliff. Like many cliff dwellings, toeholds and handholds for climbing are often found in the surrounding rock.

Poncho House, Navajo Reservation, Colorado Plateau, A.D. 1200.
Located at the base of a massive cliff overlooking parts of Monument Valley and protected from the elements, the Poncho House Ruin complex is an interesting collection of striking architectural features, all carefully nestled into impressive natural-stone surroundings.

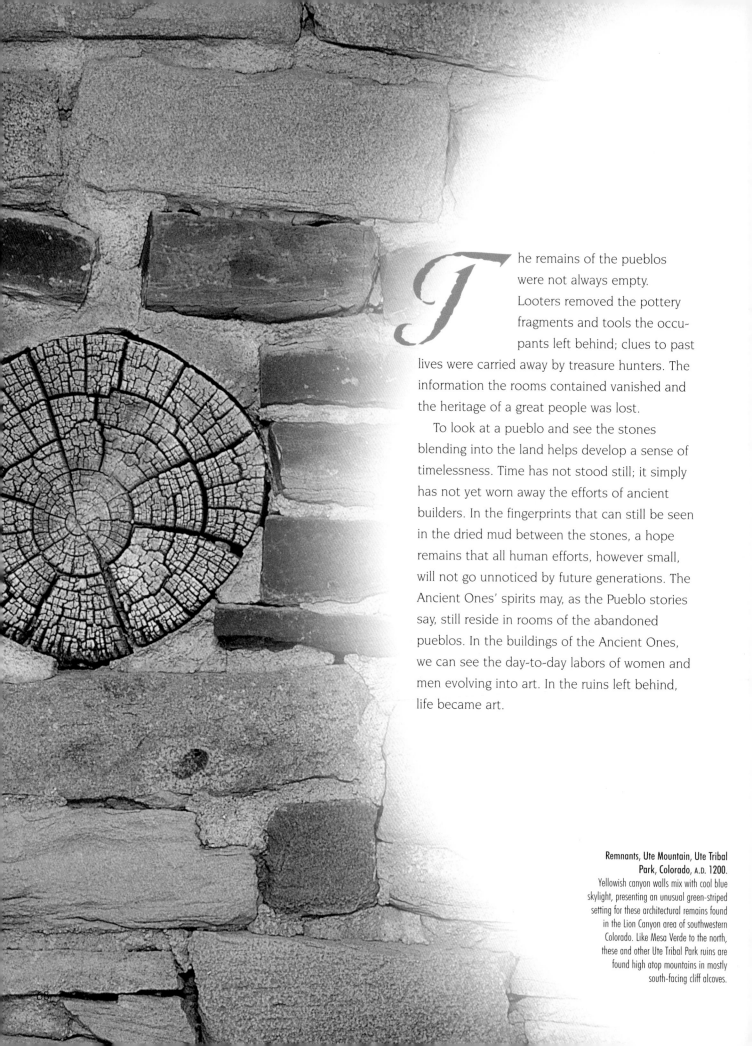

The remains of the pueblos were not always empty. Looters removed the pottery fragments and tools the occupants left behind; clues to past lives were carried away by treasure hunters. The information the rooms contained vanished and the heritage of a great people was lost.

To look at a pueblo and see the stones blending into the land helps develop a sense of timelessness. Time has not stood still; it simply has not yet worn away the efforts of ancient builders. In the fingerprints that can still be seen in the dried mud between the stones, a hope remains that all human efforts, however small, will not go unnoticed by future generations. The Ancient Ones' spirits may, as the Pueblo stories say, still reside in rooms of the abandoned pueblos. In the buildings of the Ancient Ones, we can see the day-to-day labors of women and men evolving into art. In the ruins left behind, life became art.

Remnants, Ute Mountain, Ute Tribal Park, Colorado, A.D. 1200.
Yellowish canyon walls mix with cool blue skylight, presenting an unusual green-striped setting for these architectural remains found in the Lion Canyon area of southwestern Colorado. Like Mesa Verde to the north, these and other Ute Tribal Park ruins are found high atop mountains in mostly south-facing cliff alcoves.

Eagle's Nest, Ute Mountain, Ute Tribal Park, Colorado, A.D. 1200.
Sitting on the ledge of a high cliff alcove, the exterior walls of this fortress-like structure reflect the warm light of a high canyon sunrise. This and all other ruins at the Ute Tribal Park remain in their natural, unstabilized condition, unlike those at nearby Mesa Verde.

When Clyde Kluckhohn, a scholar and traveler, caught his first glimpse of Inscription Rock, or El Morro, in 1923, he felt a sense of delight at seeing its white fortress-like walls. Kluckhohn tied his horse next to the walls of the cliff and examined the petroglyphs and pictographs left by the Ancient Ones.[2] Kluckhohn, the future scientist, let his imagination envision the artists who passed by the place he viewed in 1923. He also envisioned the past lives of what he called "Indians" who lived in this place. For this traveler the mystery and magic captured his imagination. Today we, as modern-day visitors, still envision past lives.

Marie Wormington once said that the Southwest captures your imagination. It's possible that in a sunset or a sunrise you will see the world with fresh eyes, eyes that make you feel you are the first to view this special place. Maybe one should not be so hard on Fray Marcos, who believed he saw the Seven Cities of Cibola in the sunset near Zuni. Travelers to the ancient stone homes in the Southwest who look at the vistas and ruins come away feeling that they have glimpsed something timeless.

2 Clyde Kluckhohn, *To the Foot of the Rainbows: A Tale of Twenty-five Hundred Miles of Wandering on Horseback through the Southwest Enchanted Land* (Albuquerque: University of New Mexico Press, reprint, 1992), 26–27.

Prayer Circle #1, Canyonlands National Park, Utah, A.D. 1300. Overlooking majestic Canyon Country from high atop a desert cliff-face alcove, this archaeological site invites feelings of reverence and peace.

*P*eople have lived in the Southwest for thousands of years. Native Americans carved the stone with their tools and left their symbols, and visitors and scholars alike stand in awe of their pictures.

Imaginations are still enlivened in the shadows of ruins. Maybe this is the greatest legacy left by the Ancient Ones.

Hovenweep Castle and Star Trails, Hovenweep National Monument, Utah, A.D. 1200.
Painted by flashlight and natural moonlight, this structure sits beneath the North Star during an eight-hour exposure of the heavens. Many feel the Ancient Ones used towers like those at Hovenweep as celestial observatories or for religious and community purposes.

*T*he ruins are a refuge to those seeking silence and a reminder that all things pass. The empty homes mark endings, but the eagles soaring overhead announce new life and call on the spirits of the Ancient Ones.

People come back to the pueblos because the empty rooms remind them that whatever else took place, these people lived without the constant motion of technology. Seasons, not clocks, set time schedules, and a long time ago someone not unlike us made monuments in stone.

Square Tower Group and Star Trails,
Hovenweep National Monument, Utah,
A.D. 1200.
Unusual multistoried structures of varying sizes and shapes are common at Hovenweep. Unlike the neighboring cliff dwellings at Mesa Verde, these castle-like towers stand as sentinels at the edges of nearby shallow canyons on the Cajon Mesa. Speculation centers on their usage as lookouts, granaries, water reservoirs, ceremonial structures, or celestial observatories. Severe drought between 1275 and 1300 may have hastened their abandonment.

PHOTOGRAPHER'S NOTE

*I*n an age when everything, including time, seems to be moving so fast, the ancient ruins of the Southwest provide an escape into a timeless desert environment where the beauty and peace of nature combine with the mystery of a lost civilization. As such, these ruins remind us to slow down, ponder who we are, and reconnect with all that is important.

The photographs in this book were created for two reasons. First was the desire to respond to the magical juxtaposition of form that the Ancient Ones were so masterful in creating. Whether beneath a massive stone alcove or next to an unusual geological formation, the combination of ancient architecture, carefully placed within the natural environment provided stimulating subjects for exploration. Second was the desire to document many of the more remote ancient Native American dwellings in the Four Corners area in an effort to visually preserve these endangered treasures from the effects of time, weather, and modern man. With increasing visitation, the ruins, which have withstood eight hundred years of harsh desert wind and sun, are now threatened from being loved to death. For this reason, I have not listed specific locations for some of the more remote, unprotected, and precious sites. Though not mine to keep secret, the ruins provide a priceless glimpse into the past that must be preserved so that others can also search, discover, and find solace in these very special places of peace.

This project would not have been possible without the help and vision of many people who also felt a need to assist in the preservation of the architecture of the Ancient Ones. I would like to thank Scott Mangelson of Replicolor Lab in Salt Lake City, Utah, and Ned Warner of Profile Media in Provo, Utah, for providing scanning services. As well, I would like to thank The College of Fine Arts and Communications and The Charles Redd Center for Western Studies, both at Brigham Young University, for their financial assistance. I am also appreciative to the many helpful national park and monument personnel who gladly opened "doors" so that the photographs could be produced. Lastly, I thank my family for supporting me during the five fascinating years it took to create this work.

It is my hope that we will protect treasures such as these and take only from them a rejuvenated spirit, a concern for each other, and a reminder of the mortality of our own civilization.

VAL BRINKERHOFF
NOVEMBER 1999

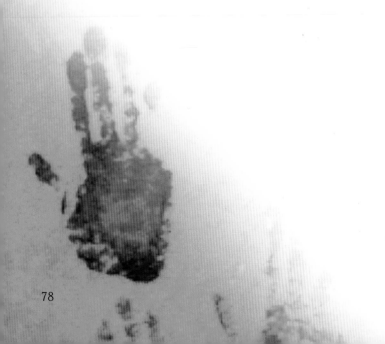

Wukoki Ruins and Star Trails, Wupatki National Monument, Arizona, A.D. 1100. Built by the Kayenta Anasazi, this stately ruin was built atop a cluster of large rocks on a small rise, surrounded by the volcanic ash spewed forth from nearby Sunset Crater. In this beautiful but desolate painted-desert and volcanic-ash environment, temperatures range from 0 to 100 degrees Fahrenheit, making water a very precious resource.

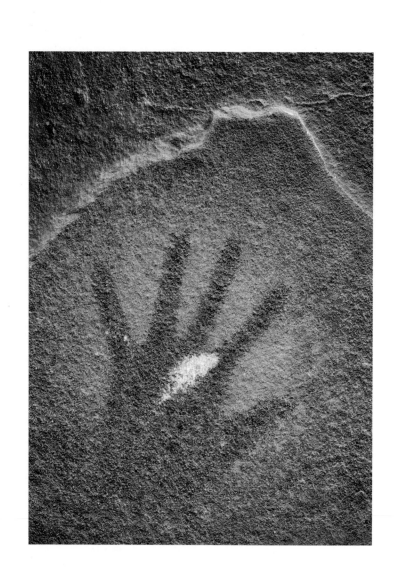